T0113703

The Student-Discussant Role
in
Doctoral Education

The Student-Discussant Role in Doctoral Education

A Guidebook for Teaching and Learning

Marie N. Fongwa, PhD, MPH, MSN, RN

Spears Books
Denver, Colorado

Spears Books
An Imprint of Spears Media Press LLC
7830 W. Alameda Ave, Suite 103-247
Denver, CO 80226
United States of America

First Published in the United States of America in 2022 by Spears Books
www.spearsmedia.com
info@spearsmedia.com
Information on this title: www.spearsmedia.com/the-student-discussant-role-in-doctoral-education

ISBN: 9781942876939 (Paperback)
ISBN: 9781942876946 (eBook)

Spears Media Press has no responsibility for the persistence or accuracy of urls for external or third-party internet websites referred to in this publication, and does not guarantee that any content on such websites is, or will remain, accurate or appropriate.

Designed and typeset by Spears Media Press LLC
Cover designed by Doh Kambem

Distributed globally by African Books Collective (ABC)
www.africanbookscollective.com

This book is dedicated to my dear late aunt and mother, Na Julia Kah Gamaga Galega, who believed in me and supported my educational pursuits.

Content

Foreword   ix

Preface   xiii

Acknowledgements   xix

Chapter One   1

   The Student-Discussant Role and Reason

Chapter Two   7

   Setting up the Stage for the Student-Discussant Role

Chapter Three   11

   Student-Discussant Role and Oral Presentation

Chapter Four   17

   Evaluating the Student-Discussant Role Presentation

Chapter Five   23

   Conclusion

Appendices   27

   Bibliography   35

   Index   37

Foreword

The Student-Discussant Role Using PowerPoint Slides in Doctoral Seminars

As a rule of thumb, human nature tends to be cynical and wary to admit whatever is considered strange or new. In academics, this is raised to the pedestal of science in philosophy designated as, the 'Cartesian Theory of Systematic Doubt', propagated by Rene Descartes. However, this is precisely, where Marie Fongwa's work: *The Student–Discussant Role in Doctoral Education* makes a departure. It supersedes the conceptual framework, since it is the result of profound knowledge, experience, and careful reflection. Her treatise concretely establishes itself as; an innovative, effective, and affective, modern academic approach of education at the doctoral level using PowerPoint slides. Above all, it has already undergone successful trial runs in several of her doctoral seminars. Consequently, by all definitions, it qualifies as a seminal production founded on firm experiential ground and headed for the stars.

Students' observations about her seminars in this respect, are significant, especially as these are in the superlative. There are those, who describe her methodology as; passionate and rewarding, encouraging, motivating with clear directives, explanations and feedbacks concluding that, "She is a superb professor". These are by no means mere flattery. Having personally been privileged to sit through some of her *student-discussant* doctoral seminars, I can attest to the fact that, they are a perfect reflection of the style, methodology and content of her presentations. These constitute some of the qualities that make her approach a palpable contribution to knowledge described as: innovative, realistic, attractive, suitable, and commendable.

To set a proper stage for such presentations, the instructor works meticulously on the selection of appropriate books and syllabi as well as, modifies the PowerPoints to stimulate, befitting student activity. The students on their part are motivated to read with keen understanding, the prescribed texts in preparation for the presentation. Thus set, the *student-discussant* role in doctoral seminars using PowerPoint slides, easily translates into a *trialogue*, tagging three components: the class, the instructor and the presenter or the student-discussant, sitting in the professorial chair and interacting with his colleagues under the mentorship of the instructor. This fortifies the *student-discussant* with enthusiasm and self-confidence against stage fright in public speaking. Ultimately, this approach stimulates class feedback, further empowering and encouraging the students through shared activity and responsibility, in one word, collegiality.

Finally, feedback and take-home messages, take the form of patterned guiding questions framed to draw out the salient points in each seminar presentation. These characterize the subject content raised by the class, interacting with the *student-discussant*. This innovative approach enables students to become better organizers, oral presenters and dispels boredom, bringing fun and excitement into the classroom. Through such collaboration, the students get to know and understand one another better. This approach equally encourages self-improvement, self-assurance, and collegiality. Accordingly, it inspires collective, active participation by the class, gives each student the opportunity to assume faculty roles, thereby preparing them for prospective teaching and professional roles at the doctoral level. Marie Fongwa's guidebook is, without a doubt a seminal production, an effective, practical, and cost-effective model for *student-discussant* education using PowerPoint slides.

Anthony Ndi, B.Ed. (Hons), Ibadan, MA, PhD, SOAS,
London
Associate Professor, Catholic University of Cameroon, Bamenda,
Cameroon

Preface

The Student Discussant-Role as a Teaching and Learning Strategy

The future of effective and committed teaching strategy in doctoral education depends on the educators of today (Oktay, Jacobson, & Fisher, 2013). As the baby boomers retire from the workforce, there is need for them to hand down innovative and effective approaches in academic teaching for the education of the next generation of nursing doctoral educators. How often have you heard of or received feedback from students with: "He or she should have just posted the PowerPoint slides online for students to review?" I heard that a couple of times before embarking on this journey about the *student-discussant* role. To me, my PowerPoint slides and my in-person presentation of them were exciting. Such feedback from my students and sometimes with low student evaluation scores on a course led me to think about the best way to stimulate doctoral students, replace boredom with active participation during the most important journey in their academic lives – acquiring much needed knowledge toward their terminal degree, specifically in the field of nursing.

The recommended textbooks with additional resource

reading lists in my course syllabi were excellent and contained current content. Besides, I spent many hours creating and updating the PowerPoint slides and additional course-related reading resources. In my student doctoral education days, I was hardly bored by what my instructors presented. This was because the instructors used PowerPoint slides together with straight talking. I took down copious notes, was focused and excited about securing a doctoral degree in the end. As I continued to reflect deeply about how best to stimulate my doctoral students, it soon jelled in my mind that times have since changed and 21st century students need updated and more challenging approaches to knowledge acquisition than the method in which I was educated.

"Dream it first before you risk take" (B. Melnyk, personal communication April 12, 2018). I have always strived for the best for my students and want them to excel! After profound refection for several days in 2013, I decided on 'inviting' the doctoral students to actively participate in what I do – 'to teach' in each of my doctoral level courses. Of course, this 'teaching' on the part of the students would not include the pedagogical conceptual frameworks or dynamics involved in the formal education of major courses for training students in the art and dynamics of teaching. However, when students 'teach' as intended here, providing them with feedback on how they handled their PowerPoint slide presentations and responded to questions from the audience (their classmates and instructor) constitute invaluable tips and feedback that students could inculcate for use in professional self-development and further innovations beyond the course in question.

I began to jot down my intuitions of how 'teaching by the

student learners' could happen and over a week of reflection figured out how the idea could be implemented. This is how the *student-discussant role* in teaching and learning came to fruition. The *student teacher* morphed into the **student-discussant**. The student is the discussant because he or she is the one who critically summarizes and presents the assigned reading on a specific topic using the PowerPoint slide presentation.

I was encouraged to try this pedagogical approach, when I reminded myself that at the department in the institution I work, a course syllabus could be revised to suit the instructor's teaching style in accordance with the course objectives. I would in no way be changing the curriculum, the course objectives, or the intended student learning outcomes by changing my teaching style, but rather, incorporating an innovative and potentially effective approach to accomplishing the course objectives in accordance with the departmental directives.

When I first used the *student-discussant* role teaching strategy, the outcome was amazing as my student evaluation scores shot up and the qualitative comments were refreshing and inspiring! It was as if I had just hit the magic teaching button. Certainly, it must have been the new approach I incorporated in what I enjoy doing most, teaching students. Some random excerpts of qualitative comments from some students were as follows:

"This was a great course. Dr. Fongwa is definitely a professional faculty member that understands the importance of engaging the working adult. She made the course interesting, meaningful and gave the right amount of assignments which allowed me to retain the information. She had realistic expectations for the class. Class was engaging, discussion was highly encouraged among the group. Workload was fair for the course load. She encouraged students to share openly their experiences. I learned and enjoyed the class. Would like for her to teach other classes within the program. I have learned so much from this course. I love how actively the student-teacher dialogue occurs in this course and that is not too much of a one-way street to facilitate the information. As an adult learner, I love the dialogue. ...Dr. Fongwa ...is an inspiration and great mentor to me. I'm looking forward to take more classes with her.[1]

The rest is history as students have indicated to me, both verbally and in writing that they learn so much from taking my courses and some wish they could take more courses with me, as their instructor. I hope the comments such as these that stimulated me as an instructor would apply to you in the same way. I knew and firmly believe that it was the effect of the *student-discussant* method of teaching and learning, that made the difference in the way the students felt about my new innovative teaching method compared to the past. Both the instructor and the students gain from using the *student-discussant* strategy. It was an amazing and humbling experience for me as a teacher particularly the student who concluded: "Thank you so much for an incredible course and experience. I hope that you can influence your colleagues to lead their courses in your footsteps. It has been the most enjoyable course we have all had."[2]

This was a pertinent and particularly touching request, which I thought should not be ignored. It was so inspirational that I felt delighted and encouraged to share this pioneering

---

1   Class report statements: Spring 2015; Summer 2017; Fall 2017; Summer 2018;

2   Class report statement: Summer 2019

strategy with colleagues, who might find themselves in similar situations. In a very significant way, it provides challenging opportunities for innovation to the course instructor.

I should therefore, immediately sound a *cautionary* note. It is to say that the *student-discussant* approach in no way takes off the weight of the teaching responsibility from the shoulders of the instructor towards his or her students. Rather, the essence of the *student-discussant* approach is to inculcate some pedagogic values in the students in an engaging manner; taking away the boredom generally associated with the tutoring technique of most instructors. Besides, adult learning requires active participation on the part of students especially, as some of them would likely assume faculty roles after graduation. As such, the course instructor's role as *facilitator* of each session of the students' oral presentation with prescribed texts places him or her on the alert with the readiness to handle pertinent intriguing *feedback*. It is therefore heavily loaded. There must be a marked feeling of progress and achievement after each presentation.

Where students have presented twice or thrice in this course during the school term, it has been observed that their performance improved progressively in subsequent presentations. The discussant role participating students are therefore not left to fend for themselves in the course, which would defeat the goal of using this strategy. The course instructor is generally ahead or stays abreast with the literature the students are required to read, which entails serious preparation on his or her part. The success of the *student discussant* methodology depends on the quality of the input and mastery of the subject content by the course instructor and his or her dexterity in managing each presentation in such a way that the participants get a feeling of progress, accomplishment, and satisfaction.

Marie N. Fongwa, PhD, MPH, MSN, RN.
Professor, Azusa Pacific University School of Nursing

Acknowledgements

This guidebook on the *student discussant* role approach came as a personal investment in deep thinking about using student feedback to improve on what I truly enjoy doing – teaching. My sincere thanks to the students who recommended that I should put my PowerPoint slides online for them to review on their own. Through the lens of the *student discussant* role in teaching and learning strategy, the PowerPoint slides in any course I teach at the doctoral level are our (course instructor and students) PowerPoint slides because we now share responsibility in the teaching and learning process. How exciting!

Thanks to my colleagues in academia who observed my teaching and gave me positive feedback and/or confirmed my true connection with the students in class in a way that brings the best out of them in the learning process. Especially noted is my colleague, Dr. Kathleen Ruccione who co-taught a course with me in 2015, confirmed that the *student discussant* role strategy was a great approach, and eventually used the method in her teaching of doctoral students. Kathleen, your astute observation and candid feedback confirmed my ingenious ability from a higher level to that of the students. Also noted is the Dean of the School of Nursing, Azusa Pacific University, Dr. Aja Lesh, for the shepherding spirit she leads with and which allows for the best professional and personal academic growth in faculty and students. Thank you Dean Lesh.

I dedicate this guidebook to my dear late aunt and mother, Na Julia Kah Gamaga Galega, who believed in me being a learner in a family where she could not find a comparable child with doing schoolwork. Mama, the pearl you observed in me has morphed into teaching what I learned to doctoral-level students via an innovative method - the *student discussant* role strategy. Njikă Nă (Mungaka for thank you mother).

Chapter One

The Student-Discussant Role and Reason

The Student-Discussant Role

Each week of the academic school term, the course instructor assigns readings and modules on various topics which all students enrolled in the course are expected to undertake prior to the class session (face-to-face or online expectations are included in the syllabus) with specified deadlines. The doctoral level courses in which this author is involved, are taught through seminar-type presentation or online asynchronously. These involve extensive discussions for both the instructor and the students, usually on topics that students would have read outside the classroom prior to each session or beginning of a new week/unit in a fully online course. Methods of delivery include face-to-face, blended (partly online and face-to-face), and fully online. The student-discussant role refers to a doctoral level student's critical reading and summarizing the main points of assigned reading(s) for the entire class through PowerPoint slides presentations. Every student reads the assigned text or book chapter(s) but only the assigned *student-discussant* prepares and shares the PowerPoint slides with the class. Critical reading and analysis also include the discussant assessing whether or not the content could be applied differently and in what way. At the doctoral level, the student-discussant is also expected to attempt correlating knowledge from the reading to his/her particular research interest area and the general class interest. The latter is important because a *student-discussant* may find out that a topic under discussion, such as a theoretical framework, fits well in supporting and guiding his or her own academic research effort.

The student presents PowerPoint slides on his or her critical summary on the topic to the rest of the class participants in either a face-to-face classroom session (or via shared screen in Zoom presentation in synchronous or distance learning and teaching) or through an online threaded discussion forum. The instructor and the rest of the student-participants give the *student-discussant* immediate feedback through questions, answers, and comments. Besides, using word adjectives such as good, better, excellent, great ..., students learn from feedback such as "... your PowerPoint slides could use more white spaces, where the slides were congested with too many words. What was the *take home message* for you reading this chapter? What clinical examples could be used to illustrate what the chapter is about? How do the concepts in the reading relate to your research interest area?"

Feedback such as described above are useful to the student and usually, he or she improves in the subsequent presentations. In a sense, the course instructor *facilitates* each session of the students' oral presentation and provides them with feedback that advance their thinking or learning and makes them better. Together with the other students, the course instructor creates a friendly audience for the *student-presenter* or *discussant*. The other students give their own feedback in terms of questions, comments, and examples. The course instructor maintains a score for each presentation. In the courses, each student may earn up to five (5) percentage points for each presentation out of a total of 15 percent (for three presentations) of the total course grade for the term.

Rationale

The *student-discussant* strategy stimulates teaching and learning as well as, encourages the active participation of the student and in a way, the approach removes the 'boring' phenomenon that some students tend to have with the monotonous pedagogic and didactic approach. Adult learning requires the active participation of the students especially at doctoral level education as some students would eventually assume the faculty roles after graduation.

Indirectly, participating in the *student-discussant* role prepares the doctoral dents for future teaching and professional presentations. Students practice how to handle assigned contents understand, summarize, and condense them into main parts so as to prepare coherent PowerPoint slides on the contents (font size, clarity, visibility, and use of space on slides taken into consideration) and orally present the information in a professional manner. In the face-to-face classroom situation, it has been amazing to note how well dressed up many *student-discussants* come to class on the day they have to present!

Because the students are allowed to play the discussant role, they ipso facto share power and authority with the course instructor. The *student-discussant* 'takes control' of the classroom environment when he or she presents through responding to questions from classmates and the instructor (a safe audience). In this regard, one of my doctoral level students on a fully online course openly noted that:

> Dr. Fongwa is an excellent instructor! She required a lot of dialogue between classmates, and she remained intimately involved in the dialogues and the discussions. I really liked her prompt responses to our posts, which were always helpful and encouraging. I learned a lot in this course.[1]

Pursuing this approach, students are evaluated on the way they respond to questions and comments on their presentations by their classmates and course instructor. Thus, they use the feedback to improve themselves in future presentations. *Student-discussant* roles minimize boredom in the course. One student, in a fully online course, firmly put it this way:

> I am in disbelief that the semester is almost over. Just unbelievable where the time went...I guess, they say when you are having fun, time will pass so fast... That said, this class was truly amazing as we learned together and applied that knowledge daily and, in all settings whether home, work, school, and community.[2]

The rhetorical question may be asked if the *student-discussant*

---

1 Ibid. Summer 2019
2 Ibid. Summer 2019

strategy in teaching and learning is a replacement for the course instructor's teaching role? In other words, "Does the *student-discussant* role take off work from the instructor and dump it on the students?" "Is the course instructor dumping his or her teaching responsibility on the students by using the *student-discussant* role in teaching and learning?" One may assert the responsibility - *dumping syndrome,* if the rationale for employing the *student-discussant* strategy were to be for something other than stimulating, teaching, and learning in the students instead of 'boring' them with the instructor's usual pedagogical and didactic approach.

In a course, where students have had the occasion of making two to three times to make presentations, it has been observed that constructive feedback to students in their first presentations usually resulted in students performing better in subsequent presentations. The discussant-role students are therefore not left to fend for themselves in the course, which would defeat the goal for the use of the strategy.

Chapter Two

Setting up the Stage for the Student-Discussant Role

Preparing for the Student-Discussant Role

Outstanding *considerations* would include the following points: Appropriate textbook(s) for the course. Selection of the right textbooks; it is of utter importance to underscore the currency of information (use the latest editions as often as possible); some books may be discontinued from the required reading list because there are no newer editions.

The Course Syllabus should have clear instructions on what students are expected to do to accomplish the discussant role.

Role of the course instructor as facilitator of the *student-discussant* role process and his or her presence should be evident in the face-to-face format and threaded discussions such as providing clarifications needed in online teaching format. In the physical classroom, the instructor is there to observe, give feedback, chime-in as needed to assist the *student-discussant* or others and answer questions from the entire class.

The First Three or Four Weeks

In the semester system, the first three or four weeks are for the instructor to demonstrate to the students, what is expected each week. Everyone reads the assigned texts but only one person prepares and presents the PowerPoint slides on the readings.

Each *student-discussant* presents on one or two chapters (most) for the weekly assigned readings; meaning that there may be two or three *student-discussants* in a week when more than two chapters are assigned for that week (assigned chapters range from 2-4 per week and depend on the number of students enrolled in the course).

Class Size

The actual *class size* determines how many students can carry out presentations in a week but with not more than three presentations per session for face-to-face or online format. In the first few weeks of the semester, the instructor (role-models like the discussant) presents a general overview on the course based on the assigned readings, capturing the main points on as many of the assigned readings for the semester as possible without too much detail.

What to Expect

The main idea at this point is to give the students a flavor of what to expect from the course and it is all right to tell them that the overview only covers the main points on all, or some of the chapters because the details would come from their wider reading, critical analysis and summarizing the assigned readings would apply when they assume the discussant role.

Instructor Sets the Example

The PowerPoint slides in the first three-four weeks of the semester by the instructor set the example on the readings in a 15/16 semester week, two to three rounds, as discussants effi-ciently executed by each student in class sizes of 5 to 15 students.

Generally, the author has used three *rounds of presentations* for each of the students during a school term.

Specific University Setting

In a quarter system, the instructor may take *the first two* instead of three to four weeks to introduce the course and functioning of the *discussant role*. Depending on the class size, only two rounds may be possible for each student to take on the role.

Avoid Overloading

Students should *not be overloaded* with doing more than three rounds maximum during a 15/16-week semester because of low student enrollment in a course. The instructor may have to be creative in how to use some of the weeks that are not covered by the *student-discussant* role assignments. For instance, the instructor provides the students with *guiding questions* for assigned topics and then allows everyone to take part in discussing the possible answers during the class meeting or through a threaded discussion in an online format of teaching and learning. From the author's experience, the last two to three weeks of the semester should not have *student-discussant* role assignments.

Proper Focus

Instead, the emphasis should be on rounding up on the course content and allowing students to focus on their term papers and other assignments. In fact, the oral presentation of a term paper takes the same format as the *student-discussant* role presentation – following specified guidelines and in person presenting in the face-to-face method of teaching, through Zoom presentation in synchronous teaching or by a voice-accompanied

PowerPoint slide presentation in a threaded online discussion forum.

Chapter Three

Student-Discussant Role and Oral Presentation

The *student-discussant* role *activities prepare students* for the oral presentation of the term paper as the student would have been used to standing in front of the class or posting their own voice-accompanied PowerPoint slides in an online threaded discussion forum.

Course Schedules

In the weekly course schedule, the instructor should lay out the dates, topics, and corresponding readings (the topics could be titles for the assigned book chapters) (*See Appendix A*).

Spread Out the Readings

The assigned readings should be spread out as much as possible throughout the semester or quarter. For instance, one or two chapters from each of two textbooks may be assigned for a week. Some book chapters are short while others are long, and the instructor should factor those into the planning.

Crucial Role of Instructor

A discussant may be assigned two short chapters, or one long chapter and the two chapters may come from different textbooks for the course. Alternatively, the instructor may decide to have the class go through one assigned book before moving to the next; the course instructor is the facilitator of the discussions and knows best about the content students are to learn.

Preparation for Various Settings

Setting: A face-to-face teaching and learning setting requires a computer set up station ready for PowerPoint slides presentation (computer, projector, and screen). Online teaching and learning require preparing a voice-accompanied PowerPoint slide and posting the presentation in an assigned discussion basket such as the Forums discussion board.

Provision of Adequate Information

Students should be provided with as much information as possible in the preparation of the voice-accompanied PowerPoint slides even if it means referring them to the IMT (information and media technology) department of the institution. Many students are often quite savvy with the needed technology and should be allowed to share their knowledge with the class.

Managing Assigned Discussant Role

An important point is to cover the course content for the semester or term for the purpose of fulfilling the course objectives. With a small size class, assigning two book chapters (from the same or different books) is possible and this author has done that successfully without overwhelming the students; feedback from students confirmed that assertion.

Small Size Class

In a small size class, online or face-to-face, there is more room to reach out to each student several times than in a large class size. In the online setting, there would be fewer postings in the discussion forums, meaning that each student would have *fewer postings* to respond to in a threaded discussion than in a large size class (a minimum of three substantial posts in response to an original post in a week/unit). The *Student-Discussant Role Sign-Up Sheet* (Appendix B) comes in very handy in managing the course content that the students would need to read and discuss.

The Sign-Up Sheet

The instructor uses the sign-up sheet to adjust the assignments. The editing function of *Google Doc* allows for clean and easy adjustments such as changing from two to one book chapters and vice versa (make needed changes without leaving undesired traces). However, it is also important to instruct the students not to change the order of the assignments placed on the *sign-up sheet* by the course instructor; once they access the sign-up sheet, they are only to place their names in available assignment cells (one name for each of the presentation rounds, two or three rounds) on the Google Doc sheet. An example of a change a student may be tempted to make on the sign-up sheet is moving the chapters around or erasing another student's name and replacing it with their own. Such *an undesirable action* by a student not only disorganizes the topics from how they are laid out on the syllabus' weekly schedule but also portrays disrespect and dishonesty on the part of the student who does that.

Default on the Syllabus

Assuming that doctoral education class size tends to be small, it might be a good idea to make two chapters for each student for each of the three *discussant role* assignments the *default on the syllabus* and to use the student *discussant role assignment sheet* (Appendix B) for adjusting a large class size; meaning that the two chapters can be spread out to one chapter per student when there are many more students enrolled in the course.

Time to Prepare

It is important also to give the students *time to prepare* for the role; so, the assignment (signing up) for the role should be done in the first and second weeks of the semester when the instructor is the one responsible for presenting his or her own lecture notes.

Late Student Registration

In the case of late student registration for the course and after students have signed on for their two or three rounds of the *student-discussant* role, it is better not to ask all students to adjust their initial commitments on the readings. Rather, the *late registration student(s)* should be placed in the week/weeks after all the other students would have finished presenting their assignments. The instructor can also review the weekly/unit presentation loads and allow for one more student discussant role presentation where it is not too dense in the rounds.

Maturing on the Program

It is possible this would be from about week 11 through 13 in a 15/16-week semester; 9-10 week in a 12-week semester; and 7-8 week in a quarter system institution. Around this time in the school term or about three weeks of the discussant presentations, students would be *more acclimated to the pattern* and the way the discussant role works and they would be able to handle three presentations in a week, if needed.

Late Student Enrollment

The student who enrolls later in the course after the early enrollees have already signed up for the discussant role, will participate in the discussions of the other students' presentations until their turn comes for presentation later on in the semester. That may also mean *presenting back-to-back* as the schedule and time would allow. For instance, a student may have to present two weeks in row so as to meet the required two or three rounds of the *student-discussant* role presentations.

Student Failure to Present

When a student fails to get a *student discussant role* assignment ready for classroom presentation, in person or posting online in a threaded discussion forum, the class discussion should still go on but without the PowerPoint slides. This is because everyone in the class reads the assigned reading(s) for the week but only the *student-discussant* for the week prepares the PowerPoint slides.

Two Crucial Points for Adjustment

These two points for adjusting the assignments for the role

in a small or large class size and handling absenteeism in terms of failure to present by a student discussant are important in managing the assignment. The course instructor facilitates all the discussions including when there are no PowerPoints from students. Pre-emptive readiness for each class session is crucial (have a back-up plan in case).

What finally emerges is that proper preparation for the student discussant role by the course instructor acting as a facilitator is a serious engagement, which far from taking off the load from the shoulders of the instructor and imposing it on the student discussant instead doubles it as the instructor anticipates and previews every presentation ensuring that all the outcomes and objectives are fully met.

Chapter Four

Evaluating the Student-Discussant Role Presentation

For each student's oral presentation on the discussant role, the instructor must be present to facilitate and evaluate the presentation, discussions, and interactions on the topic. For instance, the instructor notes whether the *student–discussant* links the content to appropriate clinical practice. Still more pertinent and important in a doctoral level course, is for the instructor to check out if the student relates the content of the presentation to his or her own research interest area. Additionally, if theories are being discussed, it would be important to see that the *student–discussant* and the class are able to properly operationalize the concepts using practical examples. The course instructor would be able to identify or pick on instances such as those described here and use as feedback points for the *student–discussant*.

Appendix C is an evaluation form for use in scoring each discussant role presentation. The instructor assigns the score based on the assignment grade distribution for the course. In the sample provided here, the discussant role presentation earns the student 15% of the total course grade. So, in Appendix C, the maximum score is 5% for each of three presentations or 7.5% for two presentations towards a total of 15% of the course grade.

Strengths and Weaknesses of the Student-Discussant Role Strategy

Conquest of Stage-Fright

Students learn to focus as they summarize the assigned readings into smaller units that should be presented in less than half an hour; usually within 12-15 minutes. The students learn to present in front of a friendly audience of classmates and course instructor. This process gently takes away the *stage-fright* that some people have presenting to an audience. The *student–discussant* role strategy requires the course instructor to be constantly alert, monitoring the process. The students need to keep track of the readings they signed up for and use the right editions of the required books as some chapters are moved around in newer editions (the instructor makes all effort to use the latest edition of required textbooks).

Everything is Important

The *student–discussant* needs to stick with the assigned date and if there is a need for a date change, the instructor must be informed ahead of time so that arrangement can be made with another student willing-to-move to a different date (this is responsibility for both the student, who needs the change and the instructor, who must document the needed change as well as inform the entire class about the change). Nothing should be taken for granted – all participants' cooperation is needed for the strategy to work smoothly and when it works, almost everyone is happy.

Factor in Student Enrollment

Student Enrollment may challenge the instructor but keeping in mind the course objectives and whether or not the enrollment is low or high during a semester, or quarter system academic institution is crucial. It is important for the instructor to be anticipatory or, to be proactive, when revising the course syllabus – based on the current enrollment information, plus or minus from the course Add or Drop period, allowing for the first two to three weeks for the instructor and the last two to three weeks free of *student-discussant* role assignments so students can wrap up on the course smoothly. *The instructor should be able to joggle* the discussant role assignment sheet for the benefit of everyone including meeting the course objectives. *Nothing is written in stone,* but the instructor must be fully involved to reap the benefit of this innovative approach to teaching and learning in a doctoral program. The course instructor must be on top with keeping the information current such as books and other web-based resources.

Students Learn to Manage Things

Students become better organizers of oral presentation, and some *become creative.* Some students set up their presentations with objectives for audience/participants (e.g., learning outcomes), while others create questions for the participants. During one semester, a student designed a sort of jeopardy-like game for the class as a way to illustrate concepts in the presented textbook content. All these creative moves by the *student-discussant reinforce learning* and make it exciting and full of fun.

Self-Discovery and Collegiality

The process of discussing the course contents through the discussant role allows the students to know more about one another's strengths and support systems; this enables *increased collegiality among the students.* The process encourages students to use available university resources to boost and improve their presentation abilities. For instance, in my university, students in need of better writing ability, may seek assistance from the student ability-enhancing center such as the writing center to edit their presentations.

Highly Cost Effective

The *student-discussant* role teaching strategy is *cost effective.* It does not cost the student or the instructor any extra money besides what it takes to enroll in or teach the course. The expectation is to follow the instructions as described in this guidebook, *keep up with the assignments* and then reap the productive outcomes – student knowledge acquisition, student satisfaction with the course, and better student ratings on the course.

Doctoral programs focus on *developing researchers, not teachers.* Besides, people who have learned to teach may still not be able to transmit the information successfully (Oktay, Jacobson, and Fisher, 2013). However, in the United States, eligible doctoral nursing students who apply for and receive academic loans such as the Nurse Faculty Loan Program (NFLP) learn, through the courses to teach during their nursing education. NFLP is a Health Resources and Services Administration [HRSA] program that supports the training of nursing health professionals for the purpose of increasing the number of nurse educators) (data.HRSA.gov. 2019).

Chapter Five

Conclusion

In the study to examine the experiences of social work doctoral students by Oktay, Jacobson, and Fisher (2013), learning through experience was a main finding and conclusion. The students' experiential learning came through in three areas including (1) learning to establish authority, (2) developing an effective teaching style, and (3) integrating the broader context of social work education. This author can confidently say that doctoral students who have experienced the *student-discussant* role to teaching and learning will interpret their experiences in terms of the findings of Oktay and colleagues.

Specifically, the students read with discernment and under-standing, present like professionals (receiving and answering questions from a friendly audience, learn to establish authority as each of them takes on the role of the presenter and with *stage fright disappearing* shortly after assuming the role). Students come out expressing gratefulness for the chance to have learned a useful teaching skill. Besides, the doctoral students take pride in interpreting or relating what they have learned from the assignments to their respective research interest areas in nursing, although it is an expectation in all the courses the students take.

In line with the views of McNair and colleagues (2016), educating the 21st Century doctoral students, requires coming up with effective approaches to getting through to them. The doctoral students arrive with a *desire to learn and grow both professionally* and personally. The mentoring role in developing effective teaching skills in doctoral students is crucial. The *student-discussant* role method accords the doctoral level students most of the personal and professional *learning from their mentors*. Besides, it is an innovative and cost-effective method to keep students positively engaged in their own learning - gain their attention and active participation.

After all, doctoral education is about *adult learning,* and their active participation is needed. Learning and using the *student-discussant* role in teaching is a way to make a course student-ready in doctoral education. This author was sensitive and responsive to the students' concerns – they were less stimulated by the prior didactic approach to teaching. The *student-discussant* role strategy *takes out the boredom* from the teaching and learning efforts in doctoral education. To make a useful change in the world, "*your heart has to be in the right place*" (Rev. Leonardo Wilborn, personal communication, September 23, 2018). The author believes her heart was in the right place and time when the *student-discussant* role approach to teaching and learning strategy in doctoral education was conceived.

The *student-discussant* role fits into the general systems theoretical thinking (von Bertalanffy, 1981). The basic idea in systems thinking is that the whole is greater than the sum of its parts. There are relationships between the parts and the interconnections among the parts account for the nature of open systems and their *interactions with their environment.* The parts in a system relate to one another within the larger context of the whole. Similarly, the essential parts in a course that constitute the whole in the experience or the eventual outcome at the end of the term are the student and instructor's roles.

How the two roles interact as open human systems, determines the eventual outcome in the course – student knowledge acquisition and instructor continuing in the role. Combining the student discussant role on a carefully planned course content with the instructor's constant facilitative role, yields the desirable outcomes – student learning and satisfaction for both the student and instructor. A goal in the *student-discussant* role, where the instructor is fully engaged, is to involve the students in the planning, execution, and eventual acceptance of the new knowledge. *Shared responsibility warrants role accountability* on both sides. Here is what a student said about the continued facilitative role of the instructor:

> Thank you, Dr. Fongwa, for your in-depth response, for each student every week. It has a huge impact on me as a student in the investment I received through this course. You are one of the unique professors that have so much commitment to your teaching. God Bless you for your amazing work. I am enjoying and learning every moment of this course.[1]

My greatest yearning is to reach out, share, motivate and communicate with my students in the best ways possible and I

1   Class report statement: Spring 2021

find expressions such as this greatly inspiring and heartwarming. The magic wand here has been the adoption of the student discussant approach in touching my students as intensely as possible at the doctoral level. I could not wish for anything better as a mentor, stretching out meaningfully and successfully to my students. Indeed, I feel fulfilled.

Appendix A

Weekly Class Schedule and Assigned Readings

Date	Topic	Assigned readings
Week 1 mm/dd/yyyy	Introduction to Course: Overview	Book chapter Book chapter
Week 2 mm/dd/yyyy	Topics based on book chapters	Book chapter Book chapter
Week 3 mm/dd/yyyy	Topics based on book chapters	Book chapter Book chapter
Week 4 mm/dd/yyyy	Topics based on book chapters	Book chapter(s) *Student Discussant* Book chapter(s) *Student Discussant*
Week 5 mm/dd/yyyy	Topics based on book chapters	Book chapter(s) *Student Discussant* Book chapter(s) *Student Discussant*
Week 6 mm/dd/yyyy	Topics based on book chapters	Book chapter(s) *Student Discussant* Book chapter(s) *Student Discussant*
Week 7 mm/dd/yyyy	Topics based on book chapters	Book chapter(s) *Student Discussant* Book chapter(s) *Student Discussant*

Appendix B

Sample Student-Discussant Role Sign-up Sheet

Student Discussant Assignments

See syllabus for assignment instructions. The second and third round requires students to use a different author/book

Unit/ week	Student(s) assigned				
4	Book1 Ch 2 Start Round 1	Book 1 Ch 3	Book 2 Ch 2	Book 2 Ch 6	Book 2 Ch 7
5	Book1 Ch 7	Book1 Ch 8	Book 2 Ch 4	Book 2 Ch 8	Book 2 Ch 9
6	Book 3 Ch 1	Book 3 Ch 2	Book 3 Ch 3	Book 2 Ch 10	Book 2 Ch 11 End Round 1
7	Book1 Ch 13 Start Round 2	Book1 Ch 14	Book 2 Ch 12	Book 2 Ch 13	Book 3 Ch 4
8	Book1 Ch 10	Book1 Ch 11	Book 2 Ch 14	Book 2 Ch 15	

9	Book 3 Ch 11	Book 3 Ch 12	Book1 Ch 4	Book1 Ch 5	Book 2 Ch 3
10	Book 3 Ch 6 **End Round 2**	Book 3 Ch 6 **Start Round 3**	Book 3 Ch 7	Book 3 Ch 14	Book 2 Ch 5
11	Book 2 Ch 20	Book 2 Ch 21	Book 3 Ch 10	Book1 Ch 12	
12	Book 2 Ch 16	Book 2 Ch 17	Book 2 Ch 18	Book 2 Ch 19	
13	Book1 Ch 18	Book 1 19	Book 3 Ch 13 **End Round 3**		

Class size of 15 in a 16-week semester in Appendix B. Each student is responsible for a chapter from three different textbooks (Book, 1, 2, and 3) from week four through thirteen.

Appendix C

Student Discussant Role Presentation Evaluation Form

Date:_____

Student:_____

Item	Missing or unclear	Clear	Total earned % points
Clearly stated title and respective book chapter			
The main points in the reading are clearly stated			
Critical review of the content (such as new information to strengthen the science in the area)			
Concluding statement and or take home message			
Application to clinical practice – a typical example			

Item	Missing or unclear	Clear	Total earned % points
How the reading relates to student's research area of interest, if applicable			
Reaction to questions and issues related to presentation			
No unusual technical difficulties with retrieving and using uploaded presentation (for Online teaching)			
Total Earned Score			X/5

Maximum score is 5% for each of three presentations or 7.5% for two presentations towards a total of 15% of the course grade

Appendix D

Sample syllabus instruction on the Student Discussant Role.

Student Discussant Presentations (X% of Total Grade)
Due: *As Assigned*
Grading: X points for each presentation

Description

During the first/second week(s) of the course, students will sign up for two or three weeks/units where they will play the role of Student-Discussant. The number of times a student will be required to act as a *Student-Discussant* is determined by the number of students enrolled in the course for the school term but not more than three times.

As a Student-Discussant, students will present critical highlights on the assigned readings of the specific week/unit capturing crucial content relating to the course. In addition, students will apply learned concepts to their own research phenomenon of interest, as applicable.

A crucial point is, *"What aspect(s) of the student's research interest area falls in the realm of the concepts under discussion in the assigned reading(s)?"* In other words, the student discussant will discuss how parts of or all concepts from the specific session discussion apply to own research interest area.

All class participants are expected to provide constructive

feedback to each discussant, and the discussant should be prepared to respond appropriately. For online format students, during their time as *Student-Discussant*, students are required to monitor their discussion thread and continue to engage in the conversations/discussions/comments throughout the allotted period in the week/unit (e.g., from Monday through Friday).

Requirements

Students are expected to prepare 10-20 slides and share a 12-15 minutes presentation with the audience each time they present. A professional skill/approach to oral presentation that goes a long way in an academic career. Each student in the class would have access to each of the presentations.

Students are encouraged to choose different textbooks for each presentation they sign up for. For example, if a student has the opportunity to be a discussant twice, they will need to use different textbooks as the basis for their presentation during each turn as *Student-Discussant*.

When there is more than one chance to be a discussant, the student will present in the first, mid, and last (three chances) *or* first and last (two chances) parts of the semester.

The total assigned score for the discussant role will be divided by the number of times a student is to be a discussant. For example, if the score for three discussant role is 15% of the course grade, then each presentation is 5%.

Bibliography

Bertallanffy, v. L. (1981). Perspectives on general system theory. Brazillar.

Brookfield, S. D. & Preskkill, S. (2005). Discussion as a way of teaching. Tools and techniques for democratic classrooms. Jossey-Bass. (2nd Edition)

Data.HRSA.gov (2019). https://data.hrsa.gov/topics/grants.

McNair, B. T., Albertine, S., Cooper, M. A., McDonald, N., Major, T. (2016). Becoming a Student-Ready College: A new culture of leadership for student success. San Francisco, CA. Jossey-Bass.

Oktay, J. S., Jacobson, J. M., & Fisher, E. (2013). Learning through experience: The transition from doctoral students to social work educator. *Journal of Social Work Education*, 49, 207-221.

Index

Adult learning 3

classroom xi, 1, 2, 3, 7, 15
class size 8, 9, 13, 14, 16
clinical practice 17, 30
collegiality x, xi, 20
Conquest of Stage-Fright 18
course objectives xv, 12, 19
Course Schedules 11
critical analysis 8
critical reading 1
curriculum xv

didactic approach 3, 5, 24
discussion thread 33
distance learning 2
doctoral degree xiv
doctoral students xiii, xiv, xix,
    23, 24, 35
dumping syndrome 5

experiential learning 23

faculty roles xi, xvii, 3

Google Doc sheet 13

Health Resources and Services
    Administration 20

learning xv, xvi, xvii, xix, 2, 3, 5,
    9, 12, 19, 23, 24, 25
learning outcomes xv, 19
low student evaluation scores
    xiii

Maturing on the Program 15
media technology 12
methodology ix, x, xvii

nurse educators 20
Nurse Faculty Loan Program
    20
nursing xiii, 20, 23

online format 8, 9, 33
oral presentation xvii, 2, 9, 11,
    17, 19, 33
oral presenters x
pedagogical approach xv

pedagogical conceptual frame-
    works xiv
pedagogic values xvii
Preparing for the Student-Dis-
    cussant Role 7

qualitative comments xv

research 2, 17, 23, 31, 32
role assignments 9, 14, 19

schedule 11, 14, 15
science ix, 30
semester system 7
seminar presentation x
social work education 23
Student Discussant Assign-
    ments 28
student satisfaction 20
student teacher xv
syllabus xv, 1, 14, 19, 28, 32
systems theoretical 24

teaching xi, xiii, xiv, xv, xvi, xvii,
    xix, xx, 2, 3, 5, 7, 9, 12,
    19, 20, 23, 24, 25, 31, 35
teaching style xv, 23
term paper 9, 11
textbooks xiii, 7, 11, 12, 18, 29,
    33
trialogue x
tutoring xvii
United States iv, 20

Zoom presentation 2, 9

ABOUT THE PUBLISHER

S pears Books is an independent publisher dedicated to providing innovative publication strategies with emphasis on African/Africana stories and perspectives. As a platform for alternative voices, we prioritize the accessibility and affordability of our titles to ensure that relevant and often marginal voices are represented at the global marketplace of ideas. Our titles – poetry, fiction, narrative nonfiction, memoirs, reference, travel writing, African languages, and young people's literature – aim to bring African worldviews closer to diverse readers. Our titles are distributed in paperback and electronic formats globally by African Books Collective.

Connect with Us: Go to www.spearsmedia.com to learn about exclusive previews and read excerpts of new books, find detailed information on our titles, authors, subject area books, and special discounts.

Subscribe to our Free Newsletter: Be amongst the first to hear about our newest publications, special discount offers, news about bestsellers, author interviews, coupons and more! Subscribe to our newsletter by visiting www.spearsmedia.com

Quantity Discounts: Spears Books are available at quantity discounts for orders of ten or more copies. Contact Spears Books at orders@spearsmedia.com.

Host a Reading Group: Learn more about how to host a reading group on our website at www.spearsmedia.com

Printed in the United States
by Baker & Taylor Publisher Services